Solar Power

Ed Catherall

Silver Burdett Company

Fun with Science

Electric Power Hearing   Clocks and Time
Solar Power   Sight   Levers and Ramps
Water Power   Taste and Smell Magnets
Wind Power   Touch   Wheels

First published in 1981 by Wayland Publishers Limited
49 Lansdowne Place, Hove, East Sussex BN3 1HF, England

© Copyright 1981 Wayland Publishers Limited
Published in the United States by
Silver Burdett Company, Morristown, N.J. 1982 Printing

ISBN 0-382-06627-8
Library of Congress Catalog Card No. 81-86269

Illustrated by Ted Draper
Designed and typeset by DP Press Limited, Sevenoaks, Kent
Printed in Italy by G. Canale & C.S.p.A., Turin

Contents

Our sun and sunglasses

Never look directly at the sun as it will damage your eyes.
Even the glare on a bright, sunny day will tire your eyes.

Look at a friend's eyes.
Draw what you see.
Which part is the pupil?

Ask your friend to look at a dark, shaded area. What happens to the pupils of your friend's eyes?

Now ask your friend to look at a bright, sunny area. Notice the change in the size of the pupil.

In the strong sunlight we use sunglasses or goggles to protect our eyes.

There are many different kinds of sunglasses.
What kinds do you know?
How do they protect our eyes?

Our eye

Eye lid

Pupil

Iris

Lash

4

What is sunlight?

Sunlight contains some rays that we can see and
others that we cannot.

Stand a glass full of water on a window sill in bright
sunlight.
Place a large sheet of white paper below the
window sill.
Move the paper until you see a rainbow.
Try to identify the different colours.

A natural rainbow is formed by sunlight passing
through water.

If sunlight passes through falling rain drops at a
certain angle, the sunlight splits up into its rainbow
colours.
Glass can also split sunlight into its rainbow colours.
Have you ever seen glass do this?

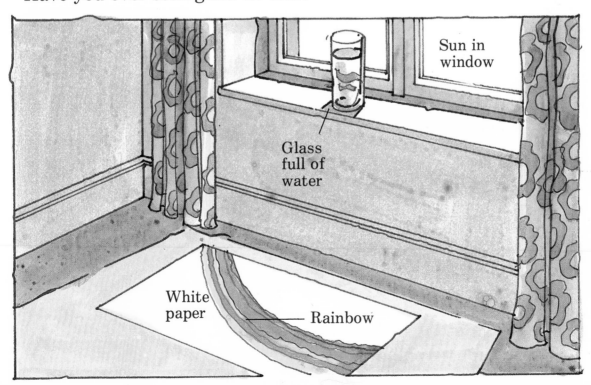

Sun in
window

Glass
full of
water

White
paper

Rainbow

Which of the sun's rays give us a sun tan?

Besides the rainbow colours, the sun's rays contain two rays that we cannot see.
We call these rays ultra violet and infra red.

The ultra violet rays affect the skin and give us a sun tan.
Too much strong sunlight is bad for our skin, so the skin darkens to stop the rays from entering it.

There are many kinds of screen sun tan products that cut down the amount of sunlight reaching our skin.

Infra red rays are the heat rays; these are the rays that burn our skin. These rays are very dangerous and you have to be very careful to avoid burns.

Many sun tan oils and lotions help you do this.

Sun tan oils and lotions also prevent the sun's rays from drying our skin.

Which sun tan oil or lotion do you use?

Cooling our body

Our body temperature is 37°C (310° Kelvin).

If the temperature outside goes above 27°C in the shade, our body feels the need to cool itself.

The blood vessels in our skin enlarge and more blood is pumped through the skin. This is to allow the air to cool the blood.

At this time our body appears flushed.

Sweat glands in the skin form sweat which stays on the body surface.
As this sweat evaporates the body cools.

To help this to happen, you often try to stand in a cool breeze.

If you get very hot, it is nice to cool the body down with a shower or to go for a swim.

To keep the body cool, you wear light, loose clothes. What are your favourite summer clothes?

Deserts

About one-fifth of the Earth's land is desert.
Deserts are dry places.
There are cold deserts and hot deserts.
Do you know the names of any deserts?
Where are these deserts?

Desert plants have tough skins and small leaves to
prevent them losing water.

There are very few large animals in a desert.
Most animals are small.
They shelter during the hot day and come out only at
night when it is cool and sometimes damp with dew.

If you are ever lost in a hot desert, learn to survive
like the animals that live there.
Find shelter from the heat of the sun.
Conserve your water.
Move as little as possible and then only at night.
Stay where you can be rescued.
Try to make things easy for your rescuers.
How would you do this?

Chapter 2 Solar heating

How much warmer do things get in sunlight than in the shade?

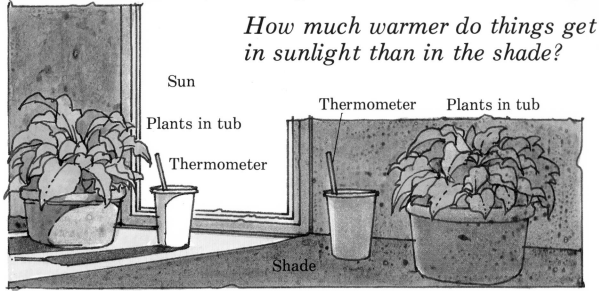

Sun

Plants in tub

Thermometer

Thermometer

Plants in tub

Shade

On a hot, sunny day, use a thermometer to measure the temperature of the ground in the sun and in the shade.
Notice how much hotter the ground is in the sun.

Pour equal amounts of cold water into two identical styrofoam cups.
Put a thermometer into each cup.
Place one cup in the sun and the other in the shade.

What is the temperature of the water in each cup after five, ten and fifteen minutes?

What would happen if you did this experiment on a cold but sunny day?

Would the water in the cup get warm on a cloudy day?

Look at plants growing in sunny areas.
Look at plants growing in the shade.
What differences can you see in the plants?

Greenhouses

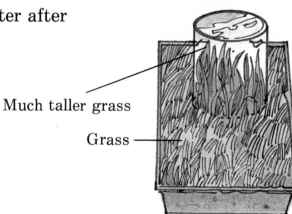

Glass jar

Put two thermometers in the sun.
Cover one thermometer with a glass jar.

After ten minutes, compare the temperatures.
Is it hotter under the glass jar?

Pour equal amounts of cold water into two
styrofoam cups.

Put a thermometer into each cup.
Place the styrofoam cups in the sun.
Cover one of the cups with the large glass jar.

What is the temperature of the water after
fifteen minutes?

Grow grass in soil in a box.
Place a large glass jar over
some of the grass.
Compare how the grass grows
inside and outside the jar.

Much taller grass

Grass

A greenhouse

Light and heat rays from the
sun pass through glass.

In cold climates a lot of food
and flowers are grown in
greenhouses or under glass.

Reflections

When light hits something smooth
and shiny that it cannot pass
through, the light bounces back.
When the light bounces back
we say that it is reflected.

Mirrors are silvered to reflect light.
If you scratch away the silver, the
mirror is just a piece of glass.

Use a mirror to bounce sunlight against a wall.
Do not bounce the sunlight into anybody's eyes.

Make a large cone with aluminium foil.
Fit the cone around a paper cup.
Use sticky tape to hold the cone together.

Put an apple slice inside the foil cone.
Point the cone at the sun.
Watch what happens, but do not let your
shadow fall on the cone.

On a hot, sunny day, your apple slice will cook.

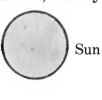

Making a solar cooker

Cut the top and front out of a strong
cardboard box.
This will be the frame of your solar cooker.

Draw a large circle on to very thick cardboard.
Measure the radius.

Cut your circle so that you have two half circles.
Cut another piece of card to hold your half
circles together.

Cover the inside of the card and the inside of the
half circles with aluminium foil.
Use rubber cement as glue.

Tape the half circles to the foil
covered card using sticky tape.
Use two nuts and bolts to fix your
solar cooker to its frame.
Make a spindle from thick wire.
Wire from an unpainted coat hanger
works well.
Push the wire spindle through the
half-radius points.

Put a sausage on the wire spindle.
Point your cooker towards the sun.
Turn your spindle to cook the sausage
evenly.

Do not touch the hot cooker or you
could get burnt.
Do not look at the reflected light in
the cooker or you could damage your eyes.

Two holes
for
bolts and nuts

Cut here
to make
two half circles

Half
radius

Half
radiu

Foil

Tape

Nut

Put stones in here
to make your
cooker stable

12

Using the sun's rays to burn paper

Put some thin paper in a metal dish.
Use a magnifying glass to focus the sun's rays to
make a small, bright dot on the paper.
How many seconds does it take before the thin paper
starts to smoke?

Measure the diameter of your magnifying glass.

Cover the magnifying glass with black paper that has
a hole cut in it that is half the size of your lens.

Focus the sun's rays again onto the thin paper.
How much longer does it take for the paper to start
to smoke?
How do you explain your results?
Could you boil a small amount of water using a
magnifying glass?

Smoke

Metal dish

6 cm magnifying glass

Black paper

3 cm hole

Paper

Is it better to use big collectors for solar power?

Find a large and a small disposable foil pie plate.
Clean each plate.
Paint each plate black using black oil paint.

When the paint has dried, put 100cc of water into each plate.
Cover each plate carefully with clear plastic food wrap.

Stand each plate on a pile of newspapers in the sun for fifteen minutes.

Now take off the wrap.
Use a thermometer to measure the temperature of the water in each plate.

For a more accurate measurement, pour the water from each plate into two styrofoam cups.

Was the water from the larger plate hotter?

Look at the clear plastic food wrap.
Why did we use this to cover the plates?

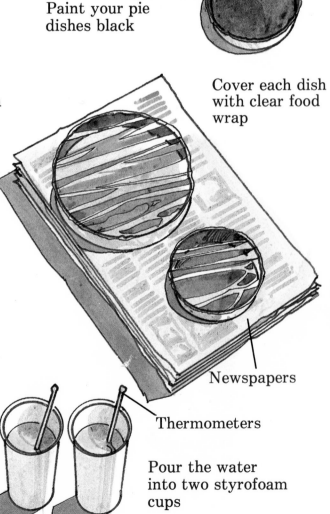

Paint your pie dishes black

Cover each dish with clear food wrap

Newspapers

Thermometers

Pour the water into two styrofoam cups

14

Which colour best absorbs the heat from the sun?

Find some sheets of coloured card.
Card that is black, white, red, blue, yellow and green would be perfect.

Cut the cards all exactly the same size.

Make some ice cubes.
Make certain that each ice cube is the same size.
Weigh each ice cube to check.

Place the sheets of card on top of a pile of newspapers in the sun.
Put an ice cube in the middle of each sheet of coloured card.

Time how long the ice cubes take to melt.
Which ice cube melted first?
Which colour absorbs most heat from the sun?
Which ice cube melted last?
Which colour absorbs least heat from the sun?
Did you find that dark colours absorbed more heat than light colours?
Would a house with a dark roof absorb more heat than a house with a light roof?

Newspapers

Ice cubes

Which material stores solar heat best?

Find a large cardboard box.
Paint the box inside and outside
with black oil paint.

Find four small, identical metal cans.
When the box is dry, make sure that
all four cans fit inside the box without
touching each other.

Fill one can with salt.
Fill another can with sand.
Fill the third can with small stones.
Fill the last can with shredded
newspaper.
Try to fill each can to the same level.

If you have enough thermometers, put
one in each can.

Place your black box in the sun.
Put the four cans inside the box
and close the lid.
Leave the box in the sun for
thirty minutes.

Now open the box and measure
the temperature of the sand,
salt, stones and newspaper.

Which material was the hottest?
Carry the tins to a place in the shade.
Which material cools the fastest?
Which material retains heat best?

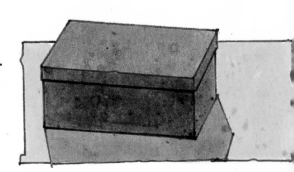

Which stores solar heat better, soil or water?

Take your large, black painted box.
Find two identical cans that fit inside
the box without touching each other.

Collect some garden soil.
Remove all the stones and dry it
thoroughly.

Fill one can with dry soil.
Put the same amount of water in the
other can.
Carefully put a thermometer into
each can.
Leave the cans in the room until they
are at room temperature.

Place your black box in the sun.
Put the can of soil and the can of water
in the box and close the lid.

After thirty minutes,
open the box and
measure the temperature
of the soil and the water.

Which heated up faster,
the soil or the water?
Put the cans of soil and
water in the shade.
Which cools faster?

Does soil or water retain
heat better?

The sun heats the land and the sea

The sun heats up the land much quicker than the sea.

On a beach in the hot sun, the sand is often too hot to walk on but the sea is cool.

At night, when there is no sun, the beach soon loses its heat but the sea keeps its heat.
The next day, in the hot sun, the sand heats up again but at night it will lose its heat.
The sea slowly builds up its heat and holds it.

In winter, the land can freeze on a cold day, but the sea is still cool.

Land temperatures can change drastically.
Siberia can be 40° C on hot summer days and minus 40° C in the depth of winter.

Britain is as far north as parts of Siberia, but is surrounded by a warm sea.
British winters are never too cold or the summers too hot.

What happens when you slowly heat water?

Find a clear Pyrex dish that will fit safely onto a gas or electric stove.

Half fill the Pyrex dish with water. Place the dish on a very low heat.

Watch what happens by looking through the sides of the dish.

Can you see the water currents rising up from the hot base?

Add a coloured bath crystal to the water. This should colour the water currents and make them easier to see.

Hot water is lighter than cold water and always rises up above cold water.

As you continue to heat the water, you will see bubbles of air form and rise to the surface.

If shallow ponds get too hot in the summer, they also begin to lose their air.
This will often make it difficult for the pond animals to survive.

Turn off the heat under the Pyrex dish before the water boils.

Heat

The sun and the ocean currents

Map of the Atlantic showing ocean currents

The sun beats down most strongly at the equator. Here the ocean is heated up and the hot water moves westward due to the spinning of the Earth. In the Atlantic the hot water moves away from Africa towards America.

When this hot water gets to the Gulf of Mexico, we call it the Gulf Stream. This hot water then flows over the Atlantic Ocean, warming Britain and preventing the sea ports from freezing in the winter.
The Gulf Stream is then cooled and goes back to the equator.

Look at a map of the world that shows the ocean currents.

See how the east coast of South America is warmed and how the west coast of Africa is cooled.

Try to find out about currents in other oceans.

Making a solar-powered fruit dryer

Find a sheet of metal gauze.
Make a wooden frame to fit the
gauze and tack the gauze in place.

Cut a piece of plywood slightly
larger than the gauze frame.
Paint the plywood black with oil paint.

Find a piece of glass the same
size or larger than the gauze frame.

Slice some apples 3 mm thick.

Place your gauze frame on top
of the black side of the plywood
board.
Use four spacers to separate the
gauze from the board.
This allows air to circulate under
the gauze.
Put the sliced fruit on the gauze.

Cover the screen with the glass.
Use another four spacers to separate
the glass from the fruit.

Place your fruit dryer in the sun.
Turn the sliced fruit every hour, as the fruit dries out
you will see moisture on the underside of the glass.
When your fruit has dried you can eat it.
Try drying different fruits; dry grapes will become
raisins.

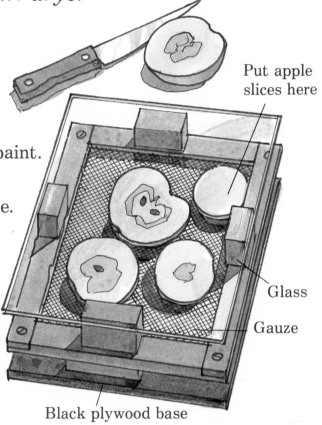

Put apple
slices here

Glass

Gauze

Black plywood base

Cover the edges of the
glass with tape to
stop it cutting your
hand.

The sun dries up water

On a hot, sunny, calm day soak two large sheets of paper in water.
Blotting paper is best but newspaper will do.

Hold up the paper and allow the extra water to drain off.

Put one sheet of paper on the ground in the sun.
Put the other sheet of paper on the ground in the shade.

Use stones on the corners to stop the paper from blowing away.

Which paper dries first?

On a hot, sunny day pour a bucket of water onto an asphalt-covered playground.
Pour some water in the sun and some in the shade.

See how quickly the wet area in the sun dries.
If you look carefully you can often see the water rising as a mist into the air.

Imagine how much of the ocean is being dried up by the sun each day.

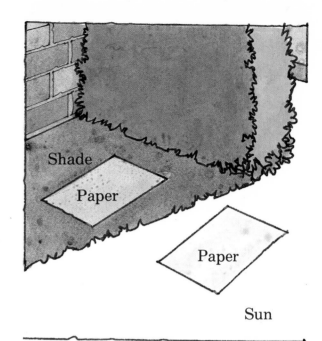

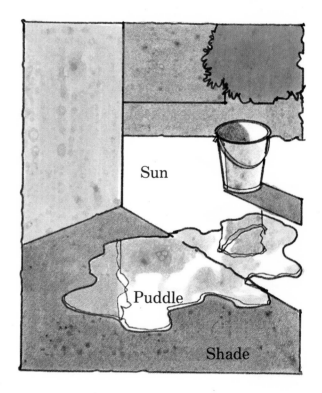

Making a solar-powered clean-water 'still'

Sun

Find a large metal pan and check it for leaks.
Fill the pan with muddy water until it is about 3 to 5 cm deep.

Place the pan in the sun.

Put a heavy drinking cup right in the middle of the pan.
See that the drinking cup does not float.
You may need to put a clean weight in the cup to stop it floating.

Cover the pan with plastic food wrap.
Tape the edges of the wrap to the pan with sticky tape.
Put a large stone on top of the food wrap to make it sag in the middle.
Do not let the food wrap touch the cup.
Check that the tape is still firmly in place.

As the sun evaporates the water, notice the clear drops forming on the plastic food wrap.

If you have placed your cup under the stone, the drops should fall into your drinking cup.

Use your still with salt water.

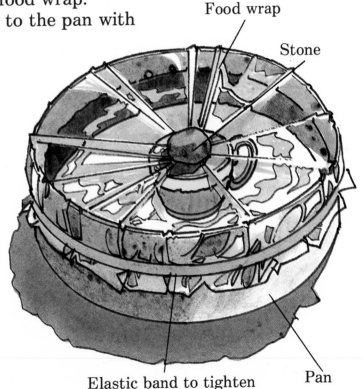
Food wrap
Stone
Elastic band to tighten the food wrap
Pan

Evaporating salt water

Make salt water by dissolving one teaspoonful of salt in a cup of water.

Find a large, flat pan.

Pour salt water into the pan until it is about 2 cm deep.

Put the pan in the sun.

See how long it takes for the water to evaporate.

When the water has all gone, see the crystals left at the bottom of the pan.

Taste some of these crystals to check if they are salt.

Look at some of these crystals through a magnifying glass.
Can you see the shape of the crystals?

In some hot countries they use the sun to make salt. They evaporate sea water in large shallow pans.

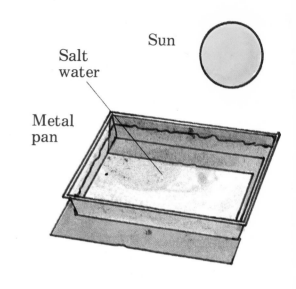

Sun

Salt water

Metal pan

Salt

Magnifying glass

24

Chapter 4 The sun as a star

Shadow sticks and sundials

On a sunny day, place a stick upright in the ground.

Mark the position of the shadow.

Mark the position of the shadow at 10am, 11am, midday, 1pm, and 2pm.

Notice that the shadows are not in the same place. This shows how much the Earth has spun.

When was the shadow shortest?
Why is this?

Notice how the shadow lengthens before and after this time.

You will get different length shadows in summer compared with winter.

It is sometimes possible to see sundials on buildings or in parks.

How does a sundial work?

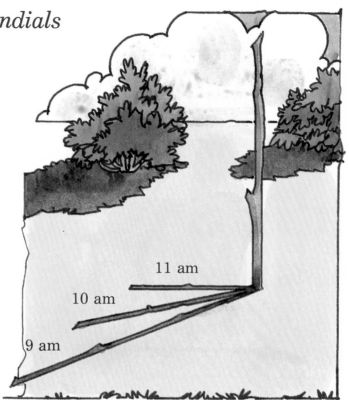

Problems with collecting solar power

Fix a magnifying glass to a chair with sticky tape.

Focus the sun's rays with the magnifying glass to make a small, bright dot on a sheet of cardboard.

Move the cardboard to get a bright spot.

Mark the position of the spot with ink.

Do not look at the bright spot or it will hurt your eyes.
Use good sunglasses to protect your eyes.

Do not move the chair or paper.
Notice how the spot of light moves.
See how soon it loses its focus.

Do this experiment at 10am, 11am, midday, 1pm, 2pm and 3pm, and see when the spot of light moves fastest?

See how fast the Earth spins.

Now you can see how difficult it is to use lenses to collect solar power.

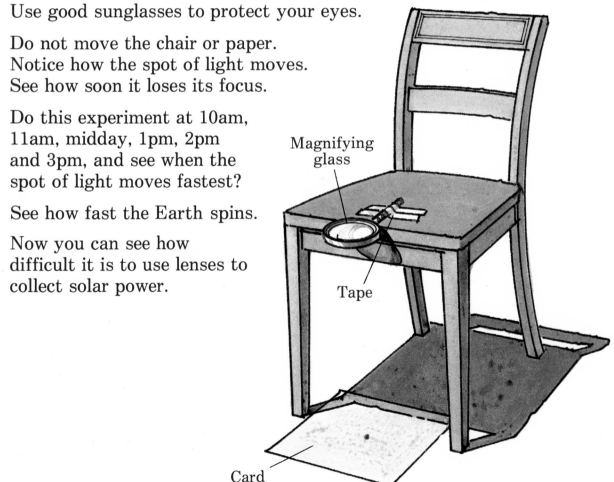

Magnifying glass

Tape

Card

Would a house get hotter if its windows faced south instead of north?

Find two cardboard boxes of the same size. Cut a large, square hole the same size on the same side of each box.

Paint each box inside and out with white oil paint.

Tape a thermometer on the floor of each box, so that you can read it when you look through the hole.

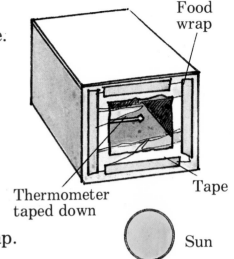

Food wrap

Thermometer taped down

Tape

Sun

Cover the holes with clear plastic food wrap. Stretch it tightly in place. Tape the plastic food wrap to the box.

Put one box facing the sun (south) and the other box facing away from the sun (north).
Record the temperature inside the boxes every ten minutes.
Do this experiment at different times of the day.

Tape a large sheet of cardboard to the top of each box to act as an overhang. See that both 'windows' are now in the shade.
What difference does this make?
Overhangs, shades or blinds are needed to stop the sun from heating a south-facing house on a hot day.

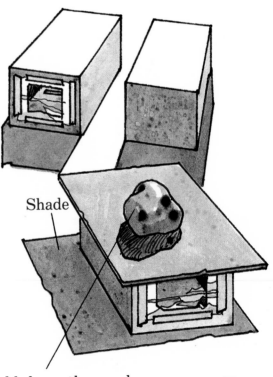

Shade

Stone to hold down the overhang

Photography

Sunlight will change many chemicals. Coloured clothes will often fade in sunlight. Some people's hair gets lighter in strong sunlight.

When we take a photograph, we let sunlight turn a silver chemical from white to black.

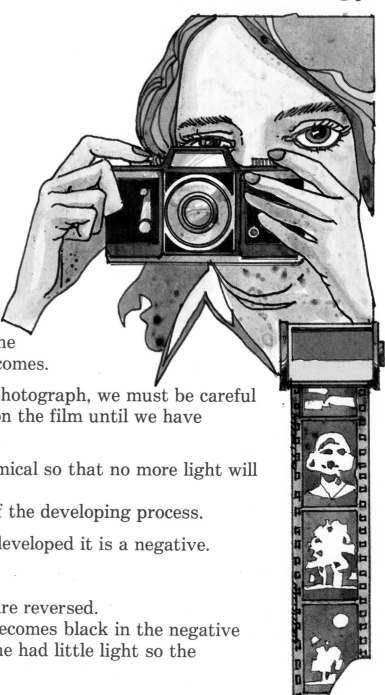

The stronger the light the blacker the chemical becomes.

When we have taken a photograph, we must be careful not to let any light fall on the film until we have preserved the picture.

We have to 'fix' the chemical so that no more light will change it.
Fixing the film is part of the developing process.

Once the film has been developed it is a negative.

Look at some negatives.

Notice how the colours are reversed.
The white in the scene becomes black in the negative and the black in the scene had little light so the chemical stayed white.

Solar cells

Connect a solar cell to an electric motor.

Hold the solar cell in the sun. How fast does the motor turn?

How hold the solar cell in the shade. How fast does the motor run?

What happens when the sun is covered by a cloud?

What is the best time of the day to get the motor to turn?

Try using the solar cell at 10am and 3pm on a clear day.

If you cannot move the solar cell during the day to follow the sun, which general direction gives the best results?

Use your solar cell inside the house.

How close do you need to get to the light from a 100 watt bulb for the motor to turn as fast as in sunlight?

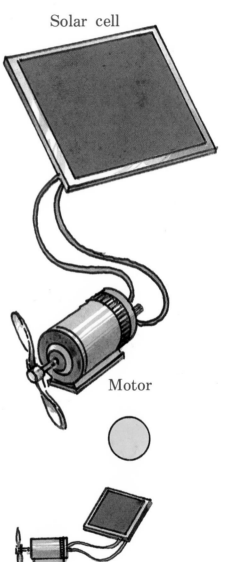

Solar cell

Motor

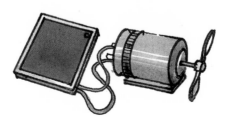

The sun gives us food

Plants take solar power and use it to make food.
Sunlight enters the green leaves of plants and the
green substance in the leaves uses it to make food.
Most of the food made is used by the plant for living.

Sometimes extra food is stored.
Food is always stored in the seed to provide food for
the new plant.

Peas and beans have a lot of food in their seeds.

Sometimes food is stored in the fruit surrounding
the seed.
You can see this in oranges, apples, pears and tomatoes.

Food is sometimes stored in special leaves, as in the
onion.
Or it can be stored in the leaf stem as in celery.

Many plants store food in their roots, such as carrots,
turnips and parsnips.

What plants have you eaten this week?

Where did these plants store their food?

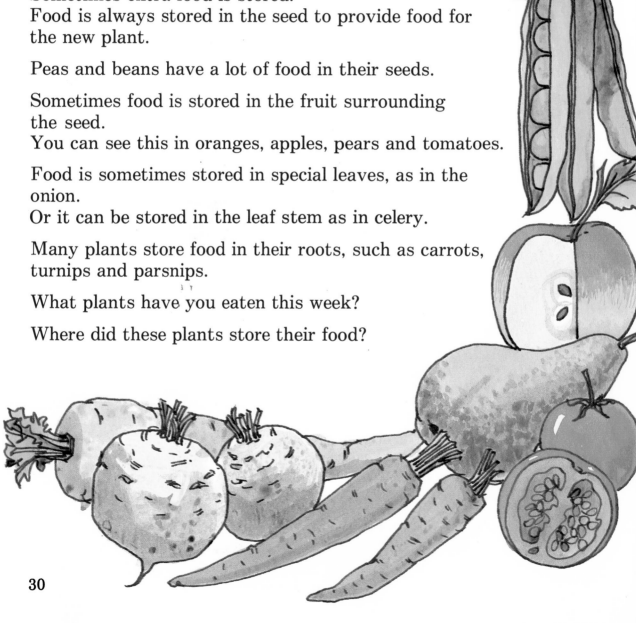

Solar power provides us with fuel

Trees use solar power to make wood.

We then take wood and burn it to provide power.

Wood burns at 270°C if it has plenty of air.
If there is not much air, it turns into charcoal, which can be burnt again.

Millions of years ago forests became fossilized.
The wood of the trees became fossils.
Coal is fossilized wood.
Coal is mined and burnt as fuel.

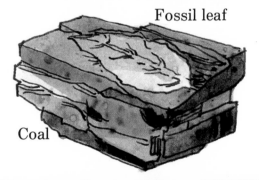

Fossil leaf

Coal

Sometimes the fossil wood was pressed under ground and it became oil.
Oil is drilled and collected.
It is too precious just to burn.
Oil is distilled into many different products.
Some of these products are petrol, gas, and oil - these are burnt.
But some oil products are used as chemicals and fertilizers.

World energy problems

No more fossil fuels are being made.
That means we are using up all the gas, coal and oil
that there is in the world.
When these are gone there will be no more.

What will we use when there is no coal to fire the
generating stations to make electricity?

What will we use when there is no gas to heat our
homes?

What will we use when there is no oil or oil products
for our cars and planes?

Now we are using nuclear power and some energy
from the wind and waves.

Can solar power be the energy of the future?

What do you think a future city will be like when
fossil fuels run out?
How will people travel?

Do you think we should try to save our fossil fuels?

How do you think this could be done?

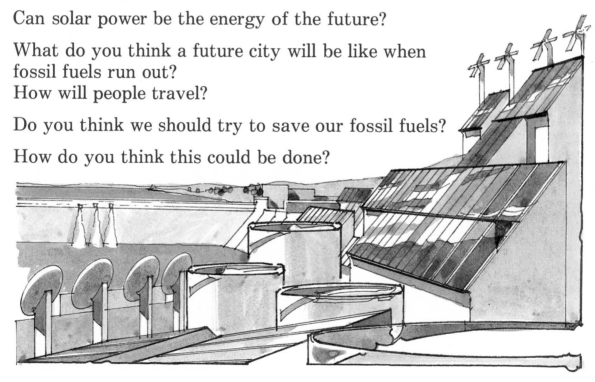

M/